# EVERYTHING YOU ALWAYS WANTED TO KNOW ABOUT STRESS...

## BUT WERE TOO NERVOUS, TENSE, IRRITABLE AND MOODY TO ASK.

### ILLUSTRATED BY: KEVIN AHERN

# WHERE WE GET THE WORD "STRESS"

THE WORD "STRESS" COMES TO US BY WAY OF
AN OBSCURE AND HAPLESS GREEK WARRIOR,
GENERAL STRESSIUS, WHO, ON THE NIGHT OF
HIS MOST DEVASTATING AND HUMILIATING
DEFEAT IN BATTLE, FOUND OUT HIS
MOTHER-IN-LAW WAS MOVING IN.

HONEY, I'M HOME!
BOY, WHAT A DAY...
HEY, WHAT'S THIS ?!!

3

# STRESS THROUGH THE AGES

SOCRATES ORDERS A DRINK. BARTENDER MESSES UP ORDER.

399 B.C.

ON THEIR WAY WEST, LEWIS AND CLARK CAN'T FIGURE OUT HOW TO REFOLD MAP.

1806

27 B.C.

1864

BEN HUR IS LATE FOR AN IMPORTANT MEETING ACROSS TOWN WHEN HE PULLS UP BEHIND STUDENT CHARIOT DRIVER.

HUH?

LINCOLN GETS TWO TICKETS TO THEATER. SOMEONE IS SITTING IN HIS SEATS.

BUFFALO BILL TAKES WRONG TURN IN GRAZING AREA, RUINS NEW BOOTS.

1872

EDISON ARGUES WITH ELECTRIC COMPANY OVER LIGHT BILL.

1885

1880

ALEXANDER GRAHAM BELL HAS IMPORTANT PHONE CALL. DAUGHTER HAS PHONE TIED UP.

1903

DURING TRIAL RUN AT KITTY HAWK, WRIGHT BROTHERS PUT IN HOLDING PATTERN.

5

# U.S. STRESS BY REGION

ROCKY MOUNTAINS: LOCKING YOUR KEYS IN YOUR LAND ROVER.

NEW YORK STATE: LOCKING YOUR KEYS IN YOUR STATION WAGON.

CALIFORNIA: LOCKING YOUR KEYS IN YOUR CONVERTIBLE.

MIDWEST: LOCKING YOUR KEYS IN YOUR PICKUP TRUCK.

TEXAS: LOCKING YOUR KEYS IN THAT GREAT BIG CAR WITH THE STEER HORNS ATTACHED TO THE FRONT.

FLORIDA: LOCKING YOUR KEYS IN YOUR RV.

HAWAII: LOCKING YOUR KEYS IN YOUR BOAT.

# STRESS: USA VS. USSR

## USA

## USSR

VISIT FROM
IN-LAWS

VISIT FROM
KGB

CHEF OVERCOOKS
K.C. STRIP STEAK

CHEF OVERCOOKS
MINSK STRIP BEETS

RUNNING OUT OF
TOILET PAPER

HEARING RUMOR OF
TOILET PAPER

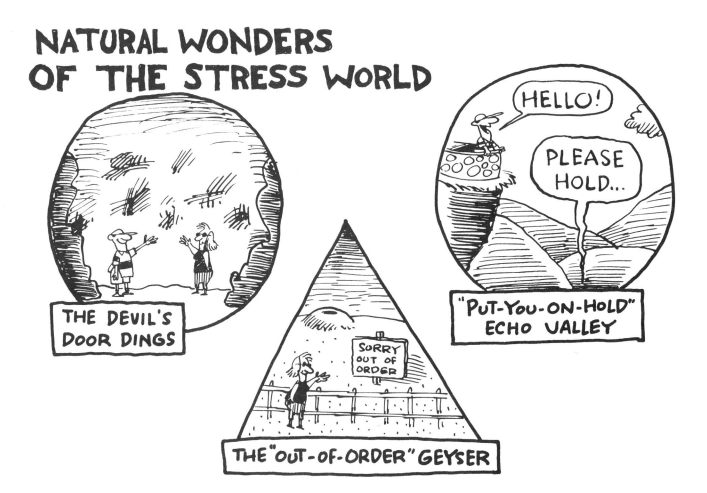

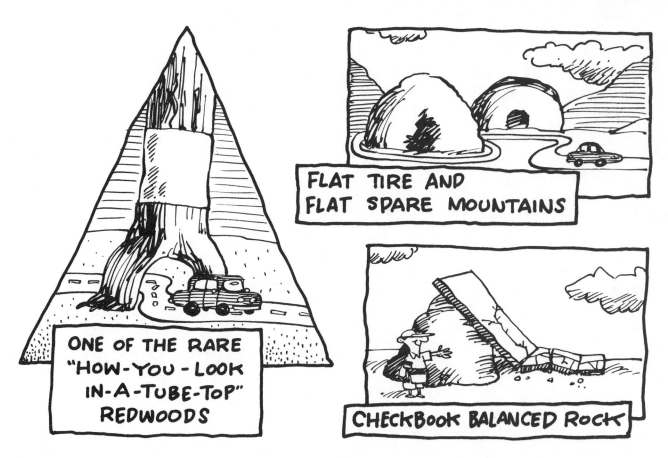

ONE OF THE RARE "HOW-YOU-LOOK IN-A-TUBE-TOP" REDWOODS

FLAT TIRE AND FLAT SPARE MOUNTAINS

CHECKBOOK BALANCED ROCK

# THE MANY FORMS OF STRESS

STRESS COMES IN MANY FORMS.
THIS IS ESPECIALLY TRUE
AROUND TAX TIME.

# WHAT PEOPLE SEE IN THIS PICTURE

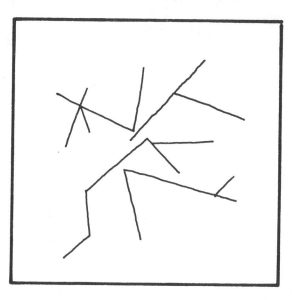

11 PERCENT: A ONE-CELLED
ORGANISM.

19 PERCENT: AN ABSTRACT
PAINTING.

70 PERCENT: THE TV SET
AFTER YOUR TEAM
BLOWS A 21-POINT
LEAD IN THE
FOURTH QUARTER.

# MOST STRESSFUL PLACES TO SCHEDULE A MEETING WITH YOUR BLIND DATE

1. CROWDED MIDTOWN BAR
2. YOUR DATE'S MOTHER'S HOUSE
3. YOUR MOTHER'S HOUSE
4. VISITOR'S ROOM AT THE PRISON

# THE LIGHTER SIDE OF STRESS

WHAT'S BLACK AND WHITE AND RED ALL OVER?

A ZEBRA WITH A BLEEDING ULCER.

KNOCK KNOCK!

WHO'S THERE?

NONE OF YOUR DAMN BUSINESS! JUST LEAVE ME ALONE AND GO AWAY!

A GUY WALKS INTO A PSYCHIATRIST'S OFFICE WITH A DUCK ON HIS HEAD. "CAN I HELP YOU?" THE PSYCHIATRIST ASKS.

SO THE DUCK SAYS, "YEAH, GET THIS IRS AGENT OFF MY BUTT!"

# DIETING

THE STRESS BROUGHT ON BY DIETING CAN OFTEN BE
RELIEVED BY STRENUOUS PHYSICAL EXERTION.
RECOMMENDED ACTIVITIES INCLUDE:

① GNAWING ON A RUBBER
   BROWNIE.

② THROWING GRAPEFRUITS AT
   PERKY SIZE 5 AEROBICS
   INSTRUCTORS.

③ PUTTING ON BLUE JEANS
   RIGHT OUT OF THE DRYER.

# WHAT'S IN THE PICTURE ?

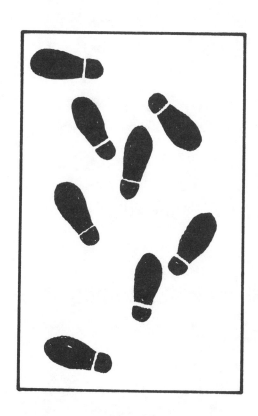

CALM PEOPLE SAY: "A FLOOR DIAGRAM USED TO TEACH THE CHA-CHA."

SLIGHTLY NERVOUS PEOPLE SAY: "TWISTER, A FUN AND CHALLENGING PARTY GAME!"

STRESSED-OUT PEOPLE SAY: "MY DOOR, AFTER I FORGOT MY KEYS ON A RAINY EVENING!"

# HIGH SCHOOL REUNIONS

THERE MAY BE SEVERAL REASONS FOR SUFFERING AN ANXIETY ATTACK WHILE GETTING READY TO GO TO YOUR HIGH SCHOOL REUNION. THEY MAY INCLUDE:

① YOU'RE WORRIED THAT YOUR CLASSMATES MAY HAVE ACCOMPLISHED MORE THAN YOU HAVE.

② YOU'RE ANXIOUS ABOUT RUNNING INTO OLD FLAMES.

③ YOU CAN'T FIND YOUR POCKET PROTECTOR.

# HOW NOT TO GET BURNED BY AN OLD FLAME

WHEN MEETING SOMEONE YOU USED TO BE ROMANTICALLY IN-VOLVED WITH, REMEMBER: THE FIRST THING YOU SAY MAY MEAN THE DIFFERENCE BETWEEN A STRESSFUL AND A STRESS-FREE MEETING. BELOW ARE SOME APPROPRIATE OPENING LINES, AND SOME INAPPROPRIATE ONES:

| APPROPRIATE: | INAPPROPRIATE: |
|---|---|
| "ARE YOU DATING ANYONE?" | "SO, WHAT POOR SAP ARE YOU BLEEDING DRY THESE DAYS?" |
| "YOU HAVEN'T CHANGED A BIT!" | "JUST CAN'T LOSE THOSE 10 POUNDS, HUH?" |
| "HOW'S YOUR LOVE LIFE?" | "STILL HAVE THOSE HEADACHES?" |

# THE TOP TEN LEAST STRESSFUL OCCUPATIONS:

10. KOJAK'S HAIRSTYLIST.
9. "ACTION NEWS" TV REPORTER IN MONTANA.
8. CRUSHING ALL THE FLAKES AT THE BOTTOMS OF CEREAL BOXES.
7. ANYTHING INVOLVING RESEARCH.
6. HEAD OF SECURITY AT THE "PEACE IN HARMONY" MONASTERY ISLAND RETREAT.

⑤ BEING PAID TO SIT IN THE BACK OF THE MOVIE THEATER AND LAUGH LIKE A DONKEY AT INAPPROPRIATE TIMES.

④ GOVERNMENT SPENDING WATCHDOG.

③ INCOHERENTLY MUMBLING OVER PUBLIC-ADDRESS SYSTEM AT AIRPORTS.

② MATTRESS TESTER.

① ANY JOB WHERE YOUR BOSS'S NAME IS "BUD."

# THE MOST STRESSFUL QUESTIONS YOU MIGHT BE ASKED AT A JOB INTERVIEW:

① "COULD YOU LEAVE YOUR RESUME AND LET US GET BACK TO YOU?"

② "WOULD YOU MIND TAKING A POLYGRAPH?"

③ "CAN YOU WORK NIGHTS AND WEEKENDS?"

④ "WHAT SIZE DO YOU TAKE IN A PAPER HAT?"

# STRESS AND PROMOTIONS

IF YOU ARE DUE FOR A PROMOTION AND THERE HAS BEEN NO HINT THAT YOU ARE ABOUT TO GET ONE, TRY THE FOLLOWING:

① A FRANK DISCUSSION WITH YOUR BOSS.
② A LETTER EXPRESSING YOUR CONCERNS TO YOUR BOSS.
③ A PHONE CALL AT 3 A.M. TO YOUR BOSS CLAIMING TO BE HIS CONSCIENCE AND TELLING HIM HE'S A SKINFLINT TIGHTWAD.

21

# STRESSFUL THINGS YOU MIGHT HEAR FROM YOUR REALTOR WHILE BUYING A HOUSE:

① "YOU LOOK LIKE A HANDY GUY."

② "TURN DOWN YOUR OFFER? NOT A GHOST OF A CHANCE... OOPS! DID SOMEBODY SAY 'GHOST'?"

③ "AND THERE'S AN INDOOR POOL, IF YOU COUNT THE BASEMENT."

# STRESSFUL THINGS YOU WILL REALIZE ONCE YOU'VE PURCHASED THE HOUSE:

# BIGGEST FEARS OF THOSE ENTERTAINING AT HOME:

① NOBODY WILL SHOW UP.

② YOU WILL RUN OUT OF SNACKS.

③ THE CONVERSATION WILL LAG, EXCEPT FOR ONE COUPLE HAVING AN ARGUMENT.

④ YOU WILL DISCOVER TOO LATE THAT YOU ACCIDENTALLY PUT SALT INSTEAD OF SUGAR IN THE DIP, AND WHEN ALL YOUR GUESTS START GAGGING AND HOLDING ONTO THEIR THROATS, YOU GIVE THEM WHAT YOU THINK IS ICE WATER, ONLY TO DISCOVER THAT IT'S REALLY A PITCHER OF VERY DRY MARTINIS, AND WHEN THEY START TO SPIT FORCEFULLY, IT WILL COMPLETELY RUIN YOUR BRAND-NEW FURNITURE, AND WEEKS LATER YOU'LL STILL BE DISCOVERING OLIVES IN REAL ODD PLACES...

# HOUSEGUEST STRESS

You know you're in for a stressful visit if your guests:

① ARE ON SOME WEIRD DIET.
② BRING PETS.
③ TRY TO AVOID LEAVING ANY FINGERPRINTS.
④ ARRIVE IN A MOVING VAN.

# TOP CAUSES OF STRESS AT HOME

 CAT

② P.M.S.

③ CAT WITH P.M.S.

26

# SURVIVING A HOLIDAY MEAL

THE HOLIDAY MEAL CAN BE A FESTIVE, JOYOUS TIME FOR A FAMILY TO GATHER AROUND A DINING ROOM TABLE. UNFORTUNATELY, STRESS CAN ENTER THE PICTURE AND RUIN AN OTHERWISE HAPPY EVENT. HERE ARE A FEW TIPS FOR AVOIDING STRESS AT HOLIDAY MEALS:

① HAVE THE CHILDREN EAT AT A CARD TABLE...IN THE GARAGE.

② BUY A TURKEY WITH 15 DRUMSTICKS.

③ EAT WITH SOMEBODY ELSE'S FAMILY.

27

# THE SUPERNATURAL...

IF YOU'RE FEELING TENSE AND UNEASY AT HOME, IT MAY NOT
BE STRESS AT ALL! YOU MAY SIMPLY BE AN UNWITTING
HOST OF THE UNDEAD! HERE'S HOW TO TELL:

| NO BIG PROBLEM | PROOF YOU'RE HAUNTED |
|---|---|
| GARAGE DOOR OPENER WON'T WORK. | GARAGE DOOR CUTS YOUR SEDAN IN HALF. |
| YOUR HEATER MAKES A "CLICKING" SOUND. | YOUR HEATER EXPLAINS HOW YOUR ANCESTORS DIED. |
| NO ONE VISITS FOR SIX MONTHS. | IN-LAWS VISIT FOR SIX MONTHS. |

# ...AND HOW TO USE IT

SUPERNATURAL PHENOMENA NEED NOT BE STRESSFUL IF YOU ACCEPT IT AS A USEFUL PART OF EVERYDAY LIFE. FOR EXAMPLE, THAT UPSTAIRS CLOSET THAT OPENS TO THE FIERY DEPTHS OF HELL CAN BE A HANDY PLACE TO HANG TOWELS SO THEY WILL BE NICE AND TOASTY WHEN YOU GET OUT OF THE SHOWER.

29

# HOME REPAIRS

TACKLING HOME REPAIRS CAN PROVE QUITE STRESSFUL. JUST REMEMBER: THE PERSON WHO TRIES TO DO IT HIMSELF IS NOT AS STRONG AS THE PERSON WHO IS ABLE TO CALL A PROFESSIONAL AND SAY, "I'M A TOTAL WIMP. TAKE ALL MY MONEY. JUST HELP ME."

# THE TERROR OF PUBLIC SPEAKING

SPEAKING IN FRONT OF AN AUDIENCE
CAN BE A NERVE-WRACKING EXPERIENCE.
IT CAN HELP TO IMAGINE THAT NONE
OF YOUR LISTENERS ARE WEARING CLOTHING.
OF COURSE, THEN YOU'LL BE FORCED TO
REALIZE THAT EVERYONE THERE LOOKS
BETTER NAKED THAN YOU DO.

# WHAT'S ON TV?

WITH SO MANY TELEVISION CHANNELS AVAILABLE TO THE AVERAGE VIEWER, IT CAN BE STRESSFUL TRYING TO DECIDE WHICH PROGRAM TO WATCH. CONSIDER THE FOLLOWING WHEN MAKING YOUR CHOICE:

1. WILL THIS PROGRAM IMPROVE MY MIND?
2. DOES THIS PROGRAM CONTAIN INFORMATION I NEED TO BE A RESPONSIBLE CITIZEN?
3. DOES THE TV LISTING SAY "NUDITY" OR MERELY "BRIEF NUDITY"?

# STRESS AND THE BIG SCREEN

THE MOST STRESSFUL THING ABOUT GOING TO THE MOVIES:

① GETTING THERE EARLY ENOUGH TO GET GOOD SEATS.
② FINDING A FILM EVERYONE WILL ENJOY.
③ GETTING THE BANK LOAN TO BUY POPCORN.

# AT YOUR LAWYER'S OFFICE

YOU SHOW UP AT YOUR LAWYER'S OFFICE WITH A LEGAL PROBLEM. WHICH OF THE FOLLOWING SIGNS ON HIS DOOR IS MOST LIKELY TO CAUSE STRESS?

# PARENT STRESS

THERE ARE REALLY ONLY TWO STRESSFUL THINGS ABOUT DEALING WITH YOUR PARENTS.

MOM AND DAD.

# DOES YOUR DOG FEEL STRESS?

IF YOU WERE FORCED TO EAT CANNED MEAT BY-PRODUCTS, DRINK FROM THE JOHN, THEN WAIT TWO HOURS UNTIL SOMEONE LETS YOU OUTSIDE, WOULDN'T YOU?

# NON-STRESSFUL BRAINTEASERS

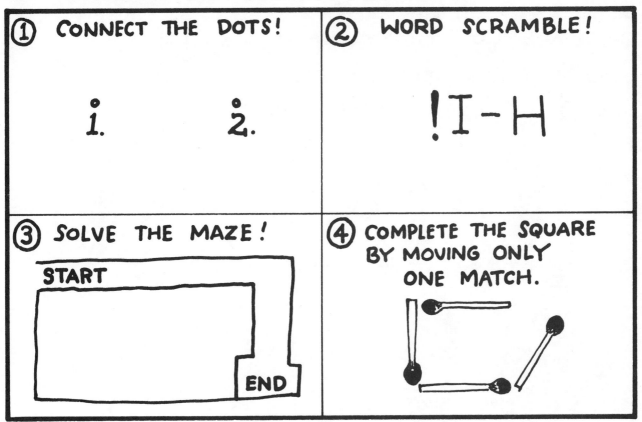

① CONNECT THE DOTS!

i.     ²̊.

② WORD SCRAMBLE!

!I-H

③ SOLVE THE MAZE!

START

END

④ COMPLETE THE SQUARE BY MOVING ONLY ONE MATCH.

# BIRTHDAYS

AFTER A CERTAIN AGE, BIRTHDAYS BEGIN TO CAUSE STRESS. THERE ARE TWO WAYS TO REDUCE THIS STRESS:

① DON'T TELL ANYONE IT'S YOUR BIRTHDAY.

② TELL NO ONE IT'S YOUR BIRTHDAY.

38

# CHECKBOOK STRESS

MANY PEOPLE FIND BALANCING A CHECKBOOK A VERY STRESSFUL EVENT. TO AVOID THIS FEELING, JUST BE SURE TO REMEMBER THESE THREE THINGS:

① ALWAYS WRITE IN WHAT YOU SPEND.

② ALWAYS SUBTRACT FROM YOUR BALANCE.

③ ALWAYS MAKE A MAD DASH TO THE BANK WITH YOUR PAYCHECK SECONDS BEFORE THEY CLOSE SO YOU CAN DEPOSIT IT TO KEEP YOUR CHECKS FROM BOUNCING.

FIRST LOCAL BANK

CLOSED

# GROCERY SHOPPING MADE EASY

THE MOST STRESSFUL QUESTION WHILE SHOPPING FOR
GROCERIES IS, OF COURSE, "WHICH LINE IS LONGER?"
THE ANSWER IS SIMPLE. ARE YOU IN IT? THEN IT'S LONGER.

# A FAVORITE STRESS RECIPE

## "MY JOB IS HELL" CIDER

FROM
MAMA STRESSKI'S
KITCHEN

1 APPLE (CORED, PEELED, AND DICED WITH AN AX)

2 CUPS OF WATER FROM THE OFFICE WATERCOOLER WITH THE GREEN STUFF FLOATING IN IT

3 TEASPOONS OF SUGAR THAT YOU HAVE TO BORROW FROM YOUR COWORKER, THE BOSS'S SPY

1 CINNAMON STICK

① IN A SMALL SAUCEPAN, OVER MEDIUM HEAT, THROW ALL THIS GARBAGE TOGETHER AND BRING IT TO A RAGING BOIL.

② LET COOL. SERVE IN A "I HATE MY JOB" MUG. GARNISH WITH SMALL UMBRELLA DRIVEN THROUGH THE HEART OF A BOSS VOODOO DOLL.

# THE MOST STRESSFUL THINGS TO HEAR AT A BEAUTY SHOP:

① "HOPE YOU LIKE HATS!"
② "WELL...IT'S ORIGINAL."
③ "DON'T YOU AGREE THAT SOCIETY OVEREMPHASIZES APPEARANCE?"
④ "MY LAWYER SAYS I'M NOT SUPPOSED TO SAY ANYTHING."

# FAMOUS STRESS QUOTES

"AT SOME POINT IN OUR LIVES, WE ALL WANT TO CHOKE OUR BOSS FOR AT LEAST 15 MINUTES." - RANDY WARHOL

"YOU CAN FOOL ALL THE PEOPLE SOME OF THE TIME, AND SOME OF THE PEOPLE ALL THE TIME, BUT YOU CAN NEVER FIND A CART AT THE GROCERY STORE THAT ROLLS STRAIGHT." -GABE LINCOLN

"I NEVER MET A DOOR-TO-DOOR SALESMAN I DIDN'T WANT TO STRANGLE." - PHIL ROGERS

43

# TOP TEN STRESSES ON THE FARM

10. ACID STOMACH IN COWS, LEADING TO AN EMBARRASSING CHORUS OF BURPS FROM THE PASTURE, AND OCCASIONALLY CAUSING A COW TO EXPLODE.

9. CROP FAILURE. ESPECIALLY WHEN IT'S TRACED BACK TO FORGETTING TO PLANT THE CROP.

8. SQUARE DANCE ADDICTION.

7. "ZIFFELITIS": PIGS WHO THINK THEY'RE HUMAN AND WANDER INTO THE HOUSE WHILE YOU'RE ENTERTAINING VISITORS.

6. SEEING YOURSELF INTERVIEWED ON "TV FARM REPORT," AND REALIZING YOU FORGOT TO REMOVE THAT GOOFY LITTLE PLAID WOOL CAP WITH THE EARFLAPS.

⑤ WILD, BLOODTHIRSTY SHEEP.
④ WORRYING IF THERE'S ANY TRUTH TO THOSE "FARMER'S DAUGHTER" JOKES.
③ HEARING A VOICE IN THE CORNFIELD SAY, "IF YOU BUILD IT, MAYBE HE'LL COME AND MAYBE HE WON'T."
② EVERY SINGLE MORNING, THAT DARN LOUDMOUTHED ROOSTER!

AND THE NUMBER ONE SOURCE OF FARM STRESS...
① DISCOVERING GRAFT AMONG THE JUDGES AT THE SO-CALLED "FAIR."

# STRESS AND THE NOISY NEIGHBOR

YOUR NEXT-DOOR NEIGHBORS ARE IN THE HABIT OF PARTYING EACH WEEKEND UNTIL THE WEE SMALL HOURS OF THE MORNING. YOU CAN DEAL WITH THIS PROBLEM WITHOUT RESORTING TO PERSONAL VIOLENCE.

DYNAMITE, TNT AND GUIDED MISSILES ARE ALL PRETTY IMPERSONAL.

# WEDDINGS

A WEDDING CAN BE A TERRIBLY STRESSFUL EVENT. ONE SURE SIGN THAT THE BRIDE IS UNDER TOO MUCH STRESS: WHEN IT'S TIME TO TOSS THE GARTER, SHE INSTEAD TWISTS IT AROUND THE NECK OF HER MOTHER.

# SWIMSUITS

THERE ARE A NUMBER OF STRESSFUL THINGS YOU MIGHT HEAR THE SALESCLERK SAY AS YOU PREPARE TO TRY ON A SWIMSUIT. AMONG THEM:

① "THE ONES WITH THE SKIRTS ARE OVER THERE."
② "ACTUALLY, IT'S NOT AS DIFFICULT TO SWIM IN A FLOOR-LENGTH ROBE AS MOST PEOPLE THINK."
③ "HA HA HA HA HA HA!"

48

# CAB STRESS

AMONG THE STRESSFUL THINGS YOU MIGHT HEAR THE DRIVER SAY WHILE YOU'RE RIDING IN A CAB ARE:

①"MIND IF WE MAKE A QUICK STOP SO I CAN CHECK IN WITH MY PAROLE OFFICER?"

②"YEAH, YOU CAN'T BE TOO CAREFUL THESE DAYS. THAT'S WHY I'M PACKING THIS!"

③"HEY! I KNOW THIS GREAT SHORTCUT!"

# THE THREE MOST STRESSFUL SPORTS:

③ GOLF

② GOLF IN SPRING

① GOLF IN WINTER

# WHAT DO YOU SEE ?

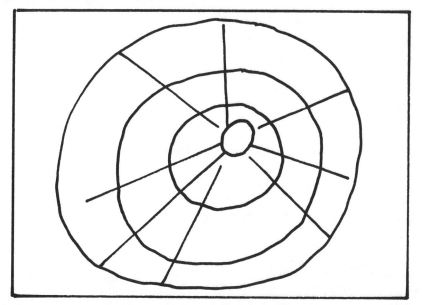

WHEN ASKED TO NAME THIS DRAWING, SOME SAID IT WAS A SPIDER'S WEB, WHILE OTHERS CALLED IT A CROSS SECTION OF A TREE LIMB. ONLY THE TRULY STRESSED KNEW IT WAS THE ARTSY DESIGN FOUND ON YOUR CAR WINDSHIELD AFTER PARKING TOO CLOSE TO A LITTLE LEAGUE GAME.

# PROFESSIONAL SPORTS STRESS

YES, YOUR FAVORITE PROFESSIONAL ATHLETES ALSO FEEL STRESS. AMONG THE THINGS THAT BOTHER THEM MOST:

1. DECIDING WHAT TYPE OF RESTAURANT TO OPEN.
2. TRYING TO SPEND 20 MILLION DOLLARS IN ONLY EIGHT YEARS.
3. THE RESPONSIBILITY OF OWNING THREE HOMES.
4. DECIDING WHICH LUCRATIVE SHOE ENDORSEMENT TO ACCEPT.
5. TRYING TO WIN ONE FOR "THE GIPPER" BUT NOT KNOWING WHAT IT IS.

# THE STRESS OF SEX

FEW THINGS ARE QUITE
AS STRESSFUL AS THAT
FIRST SEXUAL ENCOUNTER.

UNLESS IT'S NEVER
HAVING THAT
FIRST SEXUAL ENCOUNTER.

53

# STRESS AND YOUR DREAMS

THE THREE MOST STRESSFUL THINGS YOU CAN DREAM:

1. YOU ARE BEING CHASED DOWN A DARK HALLWAY BY A HOWLING MONSTER.
2. YOU ARE FALLING FROM AN AIRPLANE WITHOUT A PARACHUTE INTO A SNAKE PIT.
3. YOU ARE SPENDING A NORMAL DAY AT WORK.

# STRESS AND THE CAMPER

THREE PEOPLE AT A CAMPSITE
WERE ASKED WHAT THIS
DRAWING REPRESENTS.
HERE ARE THE RESPONSES:

**STRESS-FREE CAMPER:** "LOOKS LIKE A FAR-OFF MOUNTAIN RANGE."

**SLIGHTLY STRESSED CAMPER:** "MERINGUE TOPPING ON THE PIE I FINALLY LEARNED HOW TO MAKE IN THAT DUTCH OVEN."

**STRESSED-OUT CAMPER:** "THAT'S THE DANG CHEAP TENT THAT COLLAPSED ON ME IN THE RAIN IN THE MIDDLE OF THE NIGHT ON MY LAST CAMPING TRIP."

# YOUR MYTHS SHATTERED

AT SOME POINT IN EVERYONE'S LIFE, THEY EXPERIENCE THE TRAUMA OF REALIZING CERTAIN MYTHS ARE UNTRUE. THESE MAY INCLUDE:

① THERE IS NO TOOTH FAIRY.
② NOBODY LIVES "HAPPILY EVER AFTER."
③ THOSE THIGHS WILL NEVER BE THIN IN 30 DAYS.

# GETTING THAT DRIVER'S LICENSE

GETTING YOUR DRIVER'S LICENSE CAN BE STRESSFUL WHEN YOU REALIZE THAT:

1. YOU MAY BE QUIZZED ON THE RULES OF THE ROAD.
2. YOUR EYESIGHT MAY HAVE WORSENED SINCE YOUR LAST TEST.
3. THE TYPIST MAY LAUGH OUT LOUD AND SAY "OH, COME ON!" WHEN YOU REPORT YOUR WEIGHT.

# NEW CAR STRESS

ANYONE BUYING A NEW CAR IS BOUND TO HAVE AT LEAST ONE OF THE FOLLOWING STRESSFUL THOUGHTS:

# TRIP STRESS

THE HIGH EXPECTATIONS FOR RELAXATION ON A LONG TRIP CAN BE DEFLATED BY STRESS. HERE ARE SOME POPULAR METHODS OF RELIEVING THIS STRESS:

1. MAKE FREQUENT STOPS.
2. ADMIRE THE BEAUTIFUL SCENERY.
3. PLAY "LICENSE PLATE BINGO."
4. BRING COLORING BOOKS FOR KIDS.
5. CONSTANTLY REFER TO THE DRIVER AS A "STUPID SO-AND-SO WHO COULD GET LOST CROSSING THE STREET AND WOULDN'T KNOW A SHORTCUT FROM A COLD CUT."

# MOST POPULAR STRESS BUMPER STICKERS

# MOST STRESSFUL THINGS TO SEE WHILE COMMUTING:

① SIGN READING "CONSTRUCTION NEXT 10 MILES."

② POLICE LIGHT FLASHING IN YOUR REARVIEW MIRROR.

③ MOTHER-IN-LAW IN YOUR REARVIEW MIRROR.

④ MOTHER-IN-LAW'S REAR IN YOUR REARVIEW MIRROR.

# NO PARKING

FEW THINGS ARE MORE ANNOYING THAN ARRIVING AT A SHOPPING CENTER TO FIND THAT THERE ARE NO AVAILABLE PARKING SPOTS. YOU CAN AVOID THIS DISHEARTENING SITUATION BY :

1. ARRIVING EARLY BEFORE THE LOT BECOMES CROWDED.

2. CRUISING SLOWLY UP AND DOWN THE LANES UNTIL A SPOT OPENS UP.

3. NEVER EVER BUYING ANYTHING EVER AGAIN FOR THE WHOLE REST OF YOUR LIFE AND JUST MAKING DO WITH WHAT YOU ALREADY HAVE UNTIL IT FALLS APART AND THEN PATCHING IT BACK TOGETHER AND USING IT AGAIN UNTIL...

# JURY DUTY

OH NO! YOU'VE BEEN CALLED FOR JURY DUTY! STRESS, STRESS, STRESS! QUICK! WHAT ARE YOUR OPTIONS?

① MOVE OR GO ON VACATION IMMEDIATELY.
② RSVP AND POLITELY DECLINE. (GOOD LUCK!)
③ FORGE A NOTE FROM YOUR BOSS
   SAYING YOU CAN'T GO.
④ HIRE A LOOK-ALIKE STAND-IN.
⑤ CALL YOUR FAMILY FROM A
   PAY PHONE AND THREATEN
   THEM IN THE DEFENDANT'S VOICE.

UH, MOM...THIS ISN'T WHO YOU THINK IT IS...

# STRESS ALOFT

### THE THREE MOST STRESSFUL THINGS YOU MIGHT ACCIDENTALLY OVERHEAR YOUR PILOT SAY OVER THE INTERCOM:

# TOP CAUSES OF FLYING STRESS

① LONG FLIGHT DELAYS.

② OVERBOOKING CAUSES YOU TO GET BUMPED.

③ TRYING TO OPEN THOSE STUPID LITTLE BAGS OF PEANUTS.

# HOBBIES

SOME HOBBIES, RATHER THAN RELIEVING STRESS, CAN ACTUALLY ADD TO IT! SUBSTITUTE THE STRESS-FREE HOBBIES ON THE RIGHT FOR THE STRESS-PRODUCERS ON THE LEFT.

| HIGH STRESS | LOW STRESS |
|---|---|
| BUILDING SHIPS IN BOTTLES | BUILDING PAPER AIRPLANES IN THE DEN |
| WORKING CROSSWORD PUZZLES | WORKING CROSS WORDS INTO CONVERSATIONS |
| RIDING BICYCLES | RIDING ESCALATORS |

SKYDIVING

PIE-DIVING

# FIRST DATE STRESS

ASKING FOR THAT FIRST DATE CAN BE AWKWARD. SKIP RIGHT OVER THE STRESSFUL PART BY FOLLOWING THESE SIMPLE STEPS:

① TAKE A DEEP BREATH.

② CLEAR YOUR THROAT.

③ CHECK INTO A MONASTERY AND DEVOTE YOUR LIFE TO THE TWIN PURSUITS OF POTTERY AND CELIBACY.

WELCOME, BROTHER! ARE YOU HERE FOR THE ASHTRAY WORKSHOP?

# ELEVATOR STRESS

LIKE MOST PEOPLE, YOU DREAD GETTING STUCK ON AN ELEVATOR. THREE THINGS WOULD MAKE THIS A STRESS-FILLED EXPERIENCE.

1. THE TERRIBLE FEELING OF CLAUSTROPHOBIA.

2. THE TERRIBLE UNCERTAINTY OF HOW LONG A RESCUE WOULD TAKE.

3. THE TERRIBLE MUSIC.

# BILLS, BILLS, BILLS

WHEN IT COMES TIME TO PAY THE MONTHLY BILLS, YOUR ANXIETY LEVEL IS BOUND TO INCREASE. HERE ARE SOME SIMPLE STEPS TO MAKE BILL-PAYING A MORE PLEASANT PROCESS:

1. LOWER YOUR STANDARD OF LIVING SO FEWER BILLS COME IN.
2. PLAY SOOTHING MUSIC ON THE STEREO WHILE YOU WRITE THE CHECKS.
3. FIND THE RICHEST GUY IN TOWN AND FOLLOW HIM AROUND UNTIL THE OPPORTUNITY ARISES TO SAVE HIS LIFE.

# TAKE-OUT STRESS

HAVING A PIZZA DELIVERED TO YOUR HOUSE IS A FUN AND CONVENIENT WAY TO DINE. BUT IT DOES RAISE CERTAIN STRESSFUL QUESTIONS. THESE INCLUDE:

① CAN WE PAY BY CHECK?

② WILL THE PIZZA STILL BE WARM WHEN IT ARRIVES?

③ WILL THE PIZZA DELIVERY KID BE ABLE TO TELL FROM OUR SLIGHTLY EMBARRASSED SMILES THAT WE JUST FINISHED HAVING SEX?

# LIVING THE STRESS-FREE LIFE

JUST REMEMBER, IT IS POSSIBLE TO AVOID STRESS IN YOUR EVERYDAY LIFE. THERE ARE ONLY THREE AREAS YOU NEED TO STEER CLEAR OF:

① WORK
② HOME
③ EVERY PLACE IN BETWEEN

Other books from

SHOEBOX GREETINGS

(A tiny little division of Hallmark)

**HEY GUY, ARE YOU:** A) Getting Older? B) Getting Better? C) Getting Balder?
**WAKE UP AND SMELL THE FORMULA:** The A to No Zzzzz's of Having a Baby.
**STILL MARRIED AFTER ALL THESE YEARS.**
**GIRLS JUST WANNA HAVE FACE LIFTS:** The Ugly Truth About Getting Older.
**DON'T WORRY, BE CRABBY:** Maxine's Guide to Life.
**FRISKY BUSINESS:** All About Being Owned by a Cat.
**40: THE YEAR OF NAPPING DANGEROUSLY.**
**RAIDERS OF THE LOST BARK:** A Collection of Canine Cartoons.
**THE MOM DICTIONARY.**
**THE DAD DICTIONARY.**
**THE WORLD ACCORDING TO DENISE.**
**WORKIN' NOON TO FIVE:** The Official Workplace Quizbook.
**THE OFFICIAL COLLEGE QUIZ BOOK.**
**WHAT...ME, 30?**
**THE FISHING DICTIONARY:** Everything You'll Say About the One That Got Away.
**YOU EXPECT ME TO SWALLOW THAT?:** The Official Hospital Quiz Book.
**THE GOOD, THE PLAID, AND THE BOGEY:** A Glossary of Golfing Terms.
**THE COLLEGE DICTIONARY:** A Book You'll Actually Read!